# THE
## Prayer
## Journal
# FOR
# GIRLS

PAPER PEONY PRESS

*The Prayer Journal for Girls*
© Paper Peony Press.
First Edition, 2022

Published by: Paper Peony Press
www.paperpeonypress.com

All Scripture quotations, unless otherwise indicated, are taken from the Holy Bible, New International Version®, NIV®. Copyright ©1973, 1978, 1984, 2011 by Biblica, Inc.™ Used by permission of Zondervan. All rights reserved worldwide. www.zondervan.comThe "NIV" and "New International Version" are trademarks registered in the United States Patent and Trademark Office by Biblica, Inc.™

For wholesale inquiries contact: reagan@paperpeonypress.com

Lettering & Illustration © 2021 by Whitney Farnsworth

Printed in China

ISBN - 978-1-952842-64-1

*This journal belongs to:*

_____

_____

Thanks so much for buying our book!
For a free extra, email

**paperpeonypress@gmail.com**

and we will send something
fun to your inbox!

# hello!

Whether gifted or bought for yourself, we are so glad you now have this journal in your hands. We have prayed for you! Prayed that your time spent journaling in this book would be a time of getting to know God more and see that he hears you and he cares. We have laid out this journal in sections so that you can spend time praying for all the different people in your life as well as yourself. On the right hand side of each daily spread is a dot grid journal. Feel free to write down whatever is on your heart, hand letter a scripture memory verse or use it as a space to draw. It's entirely up to you!

There is a section in the back of the book to write down any and all prayers that God may have answered; big and small, it's worth recording it all! We hope your time spent journaling here leaves you feeling more connected to our ever-present God. Please reach out to us if there is anything we can join you in prayer for by emailing us at **reagan@paperpeonypress.com**. We would love to pray alongside you!

If you have any questions or concerns, please reach out as well and we will be sure to get back with you!

-The Paper Peony Press Team

# Prayer Requests

## PRAYERS FOR MY FRIENDS & FAMILY:

## PRAYERS FOR MY COMMUNITY:

## PRAYERS FOR MYSELF:

## Gratitude

- ○ _____
- ○ _____
- ○ _____

# Prayer Requests

DATE:    /    /

### PRAYERS FOR MY FRIENDS & FAMILY:

### PRAYERS FOR MY COMMUNITY:

### PRAYERS FOR MYSELF:

## Gratitude

- ○ _____
- ○ _____
- ○ _____

# Prayer Requests

### PRAYERS FOR MY FRIENDS & FAMILY:

### PRAYERS FOR MY COMMUNITY:

### PRAYERS FOR MYSELF:

## Gratitude

- ○ _____
- ○ _____
- ○ _____

# Prayer Requests

### PRAYERS FOR MY FRIENDS & FAMILY:

### PRAYERS FOR MY COMMUNITY:

### PRAYERS FOR MYSELF:

## Gratitude

- ○ _____
- ○ _____
- ○ _____

# Prayer Requests

DATE: / /

## PRAYERS FOR MY FRIENDS & FAMILY:

## PRAYERS FOR MY COMMUNITY:

## PRAYERS FOR MYSELF:

# Gratitude

○ _____

○ _____

○ _____

# Prayer Requests

## PRAYERS FOR MY FRIENDS & FAMILY:

## PRAYERS FOR MY COMMUNITY:

## PRAYERS FOR MYSELF:

## Gratitude

- 
- 
-

# Prayer Requests

## PRAYERS FOR MY FRIENDS & FAMILY:

## PRAYERS FOR MY COMMUNITY:

## PRAYERS FOR MYSELF:

## Gratitude

- ○ _____
- ○ _____
- ○ _____

# Prayer Requests

DATE: / /

## PRAYERS FOR MY FRIENDS & FAMILY:

## PRAYERS FOR MY COMMUNITY:

## PRAYERS FOR MYSELF:

## Gratitude

- ○ _____
- ○ _____
- ○ _____

# Prayer Requests

DATE: ___ / ___ / ___

## PRAYERS FOR MY FRIENDS & FAMILY:

## PRAYERS FOR MY COMMUNITY:

## PRAYERS FOR MYSELF:

## Gratitude

○ _____

○ _____

○ _____

# TAKE DELIGHT
## in the Lord

PSALM 37:4

# ON MY HEART

# Prayer Requests

## PRAYERS FOR MY FRIENDS & FAMILY:

## PRAYERS FOR MY COMMUNITY:

## PRAYERS FOR MYSELF:

## Gratitude

○ _____

○ _____

○ _____

# Prayer Requests

DATE:        /        /

## PRAYERS FOR MY FRIENDS & FAMILY:

## PRAYERS FOR MY COMMUNITY:

## PRAYERS FOR MYSELF:

## Gratitude

- ○ _____
- ○ _____
- ○ _____

# Prayer Requests

DATE:  /  /

PRAYERS FOR MY FRIENDS & FAMILY:

PRAYERS FOR MY COMMUNITY:

PRAYERS FOR MYSELF:

## Gratitude

- ○ _____
- ○ _____
- ○ _____

# Prayer Requests

DATE: ___ / ___ / ___

PRAYERS FOR MY FRIENDS & FAMILY:

_____
_____
_____
_____
_____
_____
_____
_____

PRAYERS FOR MY COMMUNITY:

_____
_____
_____
_____
_____
_____
_____
_____

PRAYERS FOR MYSELF:

_____
_____
_____
_____
_____
_____
_____
_____

## Gratitude

- ○ _____
- ○ _____
- ○ _____

# Prayer Requests

DATE: / /

## PRAYERS FOR MY FRIENDS & FAMILY:

## PRAYERS FOR MY COMMUNITY:

## PRAYERS FOR MYSELF:

## Gratitude

- ○ _____
- ○ _____
- ○ _____

# Prayer Requests

PRAYERS FOR MY FRIENDS & FAMILY:

PRAYERS FOR MY COMMUNITY:

PRAYERS FOR MYSELF:

## Gratitude

○ _____
○ _____
○ _____

# Prayer Requests

DATE:     /     /

## PRAYERS FOR MY FRIENDS & FAMILY:

## PRAYERS FOR MY COMMUNITY:

## PRAYERS FOR MYSELF:

# Gratitude

○ _____

○ _____

○ _____

# Prayer Requests

DATE:     /     /

## PRAYERS FOR MY FRIENDS & FAMILY:

## PRAYERS FOR MY COMMUNITY:

## PRAYERS FOR MYSELF:

## Gratitude

○ _____

○ _____

○ _____

# Prayer Requests

## PRAYERS FOR MY FRIENDS & FAMILY:

## PRAYERS FOR MY COMMUNITY:

## PRAYERS FOR MYSELF:

## Gratitude

- ○ _____
- ○ _____
- ○ _____

Blessed is the one who trusts in the Lord, whose confidence is in him.

JEREMIAH 17:7

# ON MY HEART

# Prayer Requests

DATE: / /

## PRAYERS FOR MY FRIENDS & FAMILY:

## PRAYERS FOR MY COMMUNITY:

## PRAYERS FOR MYSELF:

## Gratitude

- ○ _____
- ○ _____
- ○ _____

# Prayer Requests

## PRAYERS FOR MY FRIENDS & FAMILY:

## PRAYERS FOR MY COMMUNITY:

## PRAYERS FOR MYSELF:

## Gratitude

- ○ _____
- ○ _____
- ○ _____

# Prayer Requests

DATE: ___ / ___ / ___

## PRAYERS FOR MY FRIENDS & FAMILY:

_____
_____
_____
_____
_____
_____
_____

## PRAYERS FOR MY COMMUNITY:

_____
_____
_____
_____
_____
_____
_____

## PRAYERS FOR MYSELF:

_____
_____
_____
_____
_____
_____
_____

## Gratitude

- ○ _____
- ○ _____
- ○ _____

# Prayer Requests

DATE: / /

PRAYERS FOR MY FRIENDS & FAMILY:

PRAYERS FOR MY COMMUNITY:

PRAYERS FOR MYSELF:

Gratitude

○ _____

○ _____

○ _____

# Prayer Requests

DATE:        /        /

## PRAYERS FOR MY FRIENDS & FAMILY:

## PRAYERS FOR MY COMMUNITY:

## PRAYERS FOR MYSELF:

## Gratitude

- ○ _____
- ○ _____
- ○ _____

# Prayer Requests

## PRAYERS FOR MY FRIENDS & FAMILY:

## PRAYERS FOR MY COMMUNITY:

## PRAYERS FOR MYSELF:

# Gratitude

- ○ _____
- ○ _____
- ○ _____

# Prayer Requests

## PRAYERS FOR MY FRIENDS & FAMILY:

## PRAYERS FOR MY COMMUNITY:

## PRAYERS FOR MYSELF:

## Gratitude

- ○ _____
- ○ _____
- ○ _____

# Prayer Requests

## PRAYERS FOR MY FRIENDS & FAMILY:

## PRAYERS FOR MY COMMUNITY:

## PRAYERS FOR MYSELF:

## Gratitude

- ○ _____
- ○ _____
- ○ _____

# Prayer Requests

DATE: / /

## PRAYERS FOR MY FRIENDS & FAMILY:

## PRAYERS FOR MY COMMUNITY:

## PRAYERS FOR MYSELF:

## Gratitude

- ○ _____
- ○ _____
- ○ _____

Do not fear for I am with you

ISAIAH 41:10

# ON MY HEART

# Prayer Requests

## PRAYERS FOR MY FRIENDS & FAMILY:

## PRAYERS FOR MY COMMUNITY:

## PRAYERS FOR MYSELF:

## Gratitude

○ _____
_____

○ _____
_____

○ _____
_____

# Prayer Requests

DATE:        /        /

## PRAYERS FOR MY FRIENDS & FAMILY:

## PRAYERS FOR MY COMMUNITY:

## PRAYERS FOR MYSELF:

## Gratitude

- ○ _____
- ○ _____
- ○ _____

# Prayer Requests

DATE: /  /

## PRAYERS FOR MY FRIENDS & FAMILY:

## PRAYERS FOR MY COMMUNITY:

## PRAYERS FOR MYSELF:

## Gratitude

- ○ _____
- ○ _____
- ○ _____

# Prayer Requests

DATE: / /

## PRAYERS FOR MY FRIENDS & FAMILY:

## PRAYERS FOR MY COMMUNITY:

## PRAYERS FOR MYSELF:

## Gratitude

- ○ _____
- ○ _____
- ○ _____

# Prayer Requests

DATE:   /   /

## PRAYERS FOR MY FRIENDS & FAMILY:

## PRAYERS FOR MY COMMUNITY:

## PRAYERS FOR MYSELF:

## Gratitude

- ○ _____
- ○ _____
- ○ _____

# Prayer Requests

## PRAYERS FOR MY FRIENDS & FAMILY:

## PRAYERS FOR MY COMMUNITY:

## PRAYERS FOR MYSELF:

## Gratitude

- ○ _____
- ○ _____
- ○ _____

# Prayer Requests

DATE: / /

## PRAYERS FOR MY FRIENDS & FAMILY:

## PRAYERS FOR MY COMMUNITY:

## PRAYERS FOR MYSELF:

# Gratitude

- ○ _____
- ○ _____
- ○ _____

# Prayer Requests

DATE:  /  /

## PRAYERS FOR MY FRIENDS & FAMILY:

## PRAYERS FOR MY COMMUNITY:

## PRAYERS FOR MYSELF:

## Gratitude

- ○ _____
- ○ _____
- ○ _____

# Prayer Requests

DATE:     /     /

---

## PRAYERS FOR MY FRIENDS & FAMILY:

---

## PRAYERS FOR MY COMMUNITY:

---

## PRAYERS FOR MYSELF:

## Gratitude

○ _____

○ _____

○ _____

see how
the flowers
of the field
grow

MATTHEW 6:28

# ON MY HEART

# Prayer Requests

DATE: / /

### PRAYERS FOR MY FRIENDS & FAMILY:

### PRAYERS FOR MY COMMUNITY:

### PRAYERS FOR MYSELF:

## Gratitude

○ _____

○ _____

○ _____

# Prayer Requests

DATE:      /      /

## PRAYERS FOR MY FRIENDS & FAMILY:

## PRAYERS FOR MY COMMUNITY:

## PRAYERS FOR MYSELF:

## Gratitude

- ○ _____
- ○ _____
- ○ _____

# Prayer Requests

DATE: / /

## PRAYERS FOR MY FRIENDS & FAMILY:

## PRAYERS FOR MY COMMUNITY:

## PRAYERS FOR MYSELF:

*Gratitude*

○ _____

○ _____

○ _____

# Prayer Requests

DATE: / /

PRAYERS FOR MY FRIENDS & FAMILY:

PRAYERS FOR MY COMMUNITY:

PRAYERS FOR MYSELF:

# Gratitude

- ○ _____
- ○ _____
- ○ _____

# Prayer Requests

## PRAYERS FOR MY FRIENDS & FAMILY:

## PRAYERS FOR MY COMMUNITY:

## PRAYERS FOR MYSELF:

# Gratitude

○ _____

○ _____

○ _____

# Prayer Requests

DATE:   /   /

**PRAYERS FOR MY FRIENDS & FAMILY:**

**PRAYERS FOR MY COMMUNITY:**

**PRAYERS FOR MYSELF:**

*Gratitude*

○ _____
○ _____
○ _____

# Prayer Requests

DATE: / /

### PRAYERS FOR MY FRIENDS & FAMILY:

### PRAYERS FOR MY COMMUNITY:

### PRAYERS FOR MYSELF:

## Gratitude

- ○ _____
- ○ _____
- ○ _____

# Prayer Requests

DATE:     /     /

### PRAYERS FOR MY FRIENDS & FAMILY:

_____
_____
_____
_____
_____
_____
_____

### PRAYERS FOR MY COMMUNITY:

_____
_____
_____
_____
_____
_____
_____

### PRAYERS FOR MYSELF:

_____
_____
_____
_____
_____
_____
_____

# Gratitude

○ _____

○ _____

○ _____

# Prayer Requests

## PRAYERS FOR MY FRIENDS & FAMILY:

## PRAYERS FOR MY COMMUNITY:

## PRAYERS FOR MYSELF:

## Gratitude

○ _____

○ _____

○ _____

let us not love with words or speech but with actions & in truth

1 JOHN 3:18

# ON MY HEART

# Prayer Requests

## PRAYERS FOR MY FRIENDS & FAMILY:

## PRAYERS FOR MY COMMUNITY:

## PRAYERS FOR MYSELF:

## Gratitude

- ○ _____
- ○ _____
- ○ _____

# Prayer Requests

DATE:     /     /

## PRAYERS FOR MY FRIENDS & FAMILY:

## PRAYERS FOR MY COMMUNITY:

## PRAYERS FOR MYSELF:

Gratitude

- ○ _____
- ○ _____
- ○ _____

# Prayer Requests

## PRAYERS FOR MY FRIENDS & FAMILY:

## PRAYERS FOR MY COMMUNITY:

## PRAYERS FOR MYSELF:

## Gratitude

- ○ _____
- ○ _____
- ○ _____

# Prayer Requests

## PRAYERS FOR MY FRIENDS & FAMILY:

## PRAYERS FOR MY COMMUNITY:

## PRAYERS FOR MYSELF:

## Gratitude

- ○ _____
- ○ _____
- ○ _____

# Prayer Requests

PRAYERS FOR MY FRIENDS & FAMILY:

PRAYERS FOR MY COMMUNITY:

PRAYERS FOR MYSELF:

## Gratitude

- ○ _____
- ○ _____
- ○ _____

# Prayer Requests

DATE: / /

## PRAYERS FOR MY FRIENDS & FAMILY:

## PRAYERS FOR MY COMMUNITY:

## PRAYERS FOR MYSELF:

## Gratitude

- ○ _____
- ○ _____
- ○ _____

# Prayer Requests

DATE: ___ / ___ / ___

### PRAYERS FOR MY FRIENDS & FAMILY:

### PRAYERS FOR MY COMMUNITY:

### PRAYERS FOR MYSELF:

## Gratitude

- ○ _____
- ○ _____
- ○ _____

# Prayer Requests

## PRAYERS FOR MY FRIENDS & FAMILY:

## PRAYERS FOR MY COMMUNITY:

## PRAYERS FOR MYSELF:

## Gratitude

- ○ _____
- ○ _____
- ○ _____

# Prayer Requests

DATE:     /     /

## PRAYERS FOR MY FRIENDS & FAMILY:

## PRAYERS FOR MY COMMUNITY:

## PRAYERS FOR MYSELF:

## Gratitude

- ○ _____
- ○ _____
- ○ _____

# I CAN DO ALL THINGS THROUGH HIM WHO GIVES ME STRENGTH

PHILIPPIANS 4:13

# ON MY HEART

# Prayer Requests

## PRAYERS FOR MY FRIENDS & FAMILY:

## PRAYERS FOR MY COMMUNITY:

## PRAYERS FOR MYSELF:

## Gratitude

- ○ _____
- ○ _____
- ○ _____

# Prayer Requests

DATE: /    /

## PRAYERS FOR MY FRIENDS & FAMILY:

## PRAYERS FOR MY COMMUNITY:

## PRAYERS FOR MYSELF:

## Gratitude

- ○ _____
- ○ _____
- ○ _____

# Prayer Requests

DATE: / /

## PRAYERS FOR MY FRIENDS & FAMILY:

## PRAYERS FOR MY COMMUNITY:

## PRAYERS FOR MYSELF:

## Gratitude

- ○ _____
- ○ _____
- ○ _____

# Prayer Requests

## PRAYERS FOR MY FRIENDS & FAMILY:

## PRAYERS FOR MY COMMUNITY:

## PRAYERS FOR MYSELF:

## Gratitude

- ○ _____
- ○ _____
- ○ _____

# Prayer Requests

DATE:      /      /

## PRAYERS FOR MY FRIENDS & FAMILY:

## PRAYERS FOR MY COMMUNITY:

## PRAYERS FOR MYSELF:

## Gratitude

- ○ _____
- ○ _____
- ○ _____

# Prayer Requests

DATE: / /

## PRAYERS FOR MY FRIENDS & FAMILY:

## PRAYERS FOR MY COMMUNITY:

## PRAYERS FOR MYSELF:

## Gratitude

- ○ _____
- ○ _____
- ○ _____

# Prayer Requests

## PRAYERS FOR MY FRIENDS & FAMILY:

## PRAYERS FOR MY COMMUNITY:

## PRAYERS FOR MYSELF:

## Gratitude

- ○ _____
- ○ _____
- ○ _____

# Prayer Requests

DATE: / /

## PRAYERS FOR MY FRIENDS & FAMILY:

## PRAYERS FOR MY COMMUNITY:

## PRAYERS FOR MYSELF:

## Gratitude

○ _____

○ _____

○ _____

# Prayer Requests

DATE: / /

## PRAYERS FOR MY FRIENDS & FAMILY:

## PRAYERS FOR MY COMMUNITY:

## PRAYERS FOR MYSELF:

## Gratitude

- ○ _____
- ○ _____
- ○ _____

your word is a lamp for my feet, a light on my path.

PSALM 119:105

# ON MY HEART

# Prayer Requests

DATE: ___ / ___ / ___

**PRAYERS FOR MY FRIENDS & FAMILY:**

_____
_____
_____
_____
_____
_____
_____

**PRAYERS FOR MY COMMUNITY:**

_____
_____
_____
_____
_____
_____
_____

**PRAYERS FOR MYSELF:**

_____
_____
_____
_____
_____
_____
_____

## Gratitude

- ○ _____
- ○ _____
- ○ _____

# Prayer Requests

DATE:        /        /

## PRAYERS FOR MY FRIENDS & FAMILY:

## PRAYERS FOR MY COMMUNITY:

## PRAYERS FOR MYSELF:

## Gratitude

- ○ _____
- ○ _____
- ○ _____

# Prayer Requests

DATE: / /

## PRAYERS FOR MY FRIENDS & FAMILY:

## PRAYERS FOR MY COMMUNITY:

## PRAYERS FOR MYSELF:

## Gratitude

- ○ _____
- ○ _____
- ○ _____

# Prayer Requests

DATE: / /

## PRAYERS FOR MY FRIENDS & FAMILY:

## PRAYERS FOR MY COMMUNITY:

## PRAYERS FOR MYSELF:

## Gratitude

- ○ _____
- ○ _____
- ○ _____

# Prayer Requests

DATE:    /    /

**PRAYERS FOR MY FRIENDS & FAMILY:**

_____
_____
_____
_____
_____
_____
_____

**PRAYERS FOR MY COMMUNITY:**

_____
_____
_____
_____
_____
_____
_____

**PRAYERS FOR MYSELF:**

_____
_____
_____
_____
_____
_____
_____

## Gratitude

- _____
- _____
- _____

# Prayer Requests

## PRAYERS FOR MY FRIENDS & FAMILY:

## PRAYERS FOR MY COMMUNITY:

## PRAYERS FOR MYSELF:

*Gratitude*

- ○ _____
- ○ _____
- ○ _____

# Prayer Requests

DATE: / /

## PRAYERS FOR MY FRIENDS & FAMILY:

## PRAYERS FOR MY COMMUNITY:

## PRAYERS FOR MYSELF:

## Gratitude

○ _____

○ _____

○ _____

# Prayer Requests

## PRAYERS FOR MY FRIENDS & FAMILY:

_____
_____
_____
_____
_____
_____
_____

## PRAYERS FOR MY COMMUNITY:

_____
_____
_____
_____
_____
_____
_____

## PRAYERS FOR MYSELF:

_____
_____
_____
_____
_____
_____
_____

## Gratitude

- ○ _____
- ○ _____
- ○ _____

# Prayer Requests

DATE:        /        /

### PRAYERS FOR MY FRIENDS & FAMILY:

### PRAYERS FOR MY COMMUNITY:

### PRAYERS FOR MYSELF:

## Gratitude

- ○ _____
- ○ _____
- ○ _____

# ANSWERED PRAYERS

*"Ask and it will be given to you; seek and you will find; knock and the door will be opened to you." Matthew 7:7*

# ANSWERED PRAYERS

*"If you remain in me and my words remain in you, ask whatever you wish, and it will be done for you." John 15:7*

# ANSWERED PRAYERS

_"Therefore I tell you, whatever you ask for in prayer, believe that you have received it, and it will be yours." Mark 11:24_

# ANSWERED PRAYERS

*"Then you will call on me and come and pray to me, and I will listen to you." Jeremiah 29:12*

*"Take delight in the Lord, and he will give you the desires of your heart." Psalm 37:4*

# ANSWERED PRAYERS

*"Devote yourselves to prayer, being watchful and thankful." Colossians 4:2*

# ANSWERED PRAYERS

*"Let us then approach God's throne of grace with confidence, so that we may receive mercy and find grace to help us in our time of need." Hebrews 4:16*

# ANSWERED PRAYERS

*"This is the confidence we have in approaching God: that if we ask anything according to his will, he hears us." 1 John 5:14*

# ANSWERED PRAYERS

*"I urge, then, first of all, that petitions, prayers, intercession and thanksgiving be made for all people." 1 Timothy 2:1*